Key Lessons of
Filmmaking
For Everyone

Mahmoud Reza Sani

© 2018 Mahmoud Reza Sani

2st Print Edition (English)

All Rights Reserved. Except as permitted under the U.S. Copyright Act of 1976, no part of this publication may be reproduced, distributed, or transmitted in any form or by any means, or stored in a database or retrieval system without the prior written permission of the copyright holders and publisher.

ISBN-13: 978-1725898592
ISBN-10: 1725898594

Published by: IMOFIS
International Moving Film School
https://www.imofis.com
info@imofis.com

Translation by: Alireza Lalehfar
Cover Design by: Malihe Mirzakhanian

International Moving Film School

Dedicated to all who have chosen the cinema as their original language.

Contents

Cinema for personal enjoyment	1
Why do we want to make movies?	5
Get the necessary tools for your work	8
Where to start?	10
First Steps	14
First ideas	20
Do not forget to research	23
Use your own personal experiences	25
Is there a need for a screenplay?	27
Do not doubt yourself	30
Do not express everything together	32
Spend more time on editing	35
Cinematic time and real time	38
Create the movie in your mind	40
Narrate the present time	41
Know your living environment well	43
Be your own producer	46
Actor's role	48
Do not overlook the possibilities of sound	50
Where is music in your work?	52
How to determine the size of your shots?	54
Select the right camera location	56
Your eyes and ears make your cinema	58
What is a good movie?	60

Watch good movies over and over again	62
Find people like yourself	63
Have a certain place to present your movie	65
Avoid moving camera unduly	67
Simple and inexpensive lighting	71
Costume and stage design	73
Know your strengths and weaknesses	75
Your subject should have the capacity to become a film	76
Have a workbook	78
Do not exhaust yourself	79
Go and travel	80
Do not be afraid of new experiences	82
Video Art, beyond expectation	83
Animation and limitless imagination	84
Don't make conclusions	86
Don't waste your time on rubbish	87
You are dealing with smart audience	88
Have professional attitude	90
Don't waste time	91
Archiving and keeping movies	93
Follow your personal dreams	94
Transfer your experiences to others	96

Introduction

Cinema for personal enjoyment

I have no intention to teach the classical rules of cinema in this book since they can be learned easily in a few weeks. Learning the techniques of cinema for anyone who wants to enter this field is necessary and inevitable. If you like to take full advantage of this book then the best idea is to learn the techniques and the rules first. In this book, I will talk about personal experiences and my methods used during years of filmmaking in many parts of the world. It's obvious you have to find your own solutions and find your unique ways and methods by gaining new experiences.

In this book I do my best to tell you how to make movies for your own personal enjoyment. But at the end, it's up to you to decide what to make and what to do with it. Our mentality and concept of the world we live in is unique and different from everyone else's.

Cinema entered the realm as an expensive art from the beginning and to experience it was hard and entry in it was a difficult task and the path sometimes unattainable.

Cinema was not a universal art and did not belong to ordinary people because initial facilities were expensive to provide and only a few could operate in it if there was any return of capital. That is why cinema was placed in the hands of few capitalists and profiteers from the very beginning. Obviously the artists in this field were used more in line of productivity. It is true that entertainment was the basis of cinema, but it was just a job for those involved and the result of their hard and exhausting work was entertaining people through this fresh industry. As the industry grew, companies facilitating equipment and materials were formed and started competing to innovate and make newer and lighter equipment for this demanding global market. Extremely large cameras were eventually replaced by lightweight and portable ones, also artificial studio decorations were replaced by simple and real spaces like alleys, streets, and houses. The cinema industry found its way into different countries and movie makers tried to attract more audiences through domestic and native stories. Then cinema was faced with a wide range of spectators with different tastes, and the demand had to be satisfied. Other artists and professionals considered cinema as a great medium to tell their stories due to its large audience, and as the same, governments targeted cinema as a good forum to impose their policies. That was how new directors entered the field with distinct tendencies and various types of cinema like sci-fi, detective, horror, political, romance, animation, documentary, and so on were created.

Cinema was profitable, so the number of theaters and films increased every day, and more people were eager to enter the industry day by day. That's why companies began to produce smaller, more compact cameras for educational activities. Still, the cinema was considered as an expensive industry and could not be used as an independent and personal art until the introduction of video and a few decades later by digital industry. Homemade cameras were introduced and ordinary people showed great interest and pleasure to record their important moments of their lives. High profits and acclamation brought competition among the digital camera companies. Every day, newer models, lighter and less expensive were introduced to the market. The issue got bigger and went further with the invention of cell phones and later on companies incorporated cameras and videos in them, making filmmaking more enjoyable for the public.

The digital industry gradually made the tools available to the public to use as personal art. Digital cameras made it possible for anyone who was interested in the subject to experience and create desired effect.

Unlike other fields of art, such as painting, music, dancing, sculpture, etc. cinema as an art industry has its own unique tools and ways. The cinematic art and the cinematic industry are distinguishable in two different ways but under one common ground; the language of cinema. Entering and gaining experience in this art starts with technical knowledge followed by continuous experience.

I address those in this book who like to communicate with each other through this medium and take personal joy in making their own movies. Hope that you will benefit from the recommendations of this book.

<< 1 >>

Why do we want to make movies?

Whether you want to record memories or portray unrepeatable events to be enjoyed and viewed at different times, or just for entertainment, they all involve and require personal satisfaction and enjoyment, something to add to your private collection with joy. Maybe you want to share something important, like environmental pollution and its harmful impact; it is here when you look for the most influential communication medium. Perhaps after testing many types of mass media you find that cinema is the best way to express yourself, so that through the vast possibilities of this medium it's much easier to attract audiences and bring your own words.

If you ask a filmmaker how he became one, he would definitely say he was interested in it. Naturally having interest in doing something makes the person follow the dream and become disciplined in it. Learning the tricks of the trade and gaining experience will definitely result in achieving necessary skills.

In this new era called the age of Communication the main key is to communicate with the spectators with the fastest and the shortest way possible. Many people perhaps don't bother or don't have the time to worry about environmental issues, but showing a brief picture of a lagoon being destroyed, or bad condition of the birds living there can have direct and proper impact on people watching it and may even get the responses you were looking for. Sometimes showing a few second movie intended to convey a specific message without any additional words can have such an impact that not even multiple page writing can do. That is why social network members are on the high rise and the pace of transferring thoughts and ideas get faster and faster day by day. Obviously, in order to use this new way of communication we must first learn the language well, so we can turn our thoughts, attachments and interests into films with the least possibilities and materialistic attachments. It's safe to say that in the first step we will be the ones to enjoy it over and over, and then if inclined, we may share it with others.

Digital cameras that are now abundantly and easily accessible to everyone have turned cinema to personal art, like painting that is enjoyable and could be done alone. For making movies there is no need to undertake huge costs that existed before. Naturally, there are differences between documentaries and fictional films that we will come across in this book. To make a drawing, you only need a pencil and paper or canvas, brush and paint for oil paintings. Of course your imagination and your point of view come first. This is how you create a work of art without intermediaries. You spend hours brushing the canvas and enjoy every moment of it. When the painting is done, you see the result of your dream and your imagination objectively and share the enjoyment with others. Here you are going to create films with only a digital camera. You have no commitment to anyone because you work for yourself, because no investor is involved, and you don't have to commit to anyone but yourself. So, you start to experience new things however you like and increase your knowledge every time. You are free to use your movies in any way you like, show them wherever you like or just see and enjoy them yourself.

<< 2 >>

Get the necessary tools for your work

You need to be familiar with the tools of any profession you work in and have the skills in using them. To do this, you must first get your own tools. A carpenter needs nail, hammer and saw, painter needs brush and canvas, or hunter a gun. Here the camera is filmmaker's tool. So the first step is to get a camera. Fortunately, there are colorful choices of digital cameras available with different prices in the market to meet any budget. Let's mention once more that our purpose here is not to create high cost films to be distributed in the huge cinema industry. That type of cinema has its own definition and is not consistent with my recommendations. Obviously the tools and instruments required for this type of filming are completely different and certainly not cost effective for you and certainly not necessary here. No one can work alone in the cinema which we consider an industry since having large groups or personnel are inevitable. So let us forget about the cinema industry and move on to the independent film that will turn into personal art for us. A camera, a tripod and a personal computer (preferably a laptop) including editing software is enough to get started. You can even start with a cell phone. You do not have to spend lots of money on buying equipment because variety of equipment, prices and brands in the digital market are so colorful that can confuse any one. Also you won't hunger for newer naturally more expensive devices all the time because they make you forget your main subject and the theme. Avoid useless temptations for getting various and in many cases ineffective types of equipment. Getting acceptable sound and image that can be edited easily would be enough for you. I advise to use any tools available like a laptop or even a cell phone, that's enough for now. All it takes is to install editing software which thankfully does not cost much. These programs are easy to work with and you can learn the essential and practical tips in a matter of hours. Gradually as you get more experienced you can move up to more professional equipment. But do not bother if you are facing financial problems to purchase this professional equipment. There are many places to rent equipment too. You can finish filming within few days with a fraction of the cost with the right planning.

If your wallet allows and don't have financial problems then having a good and professional equipment from the start is a good idea and a great help, but having professional and expensive equipment is not necessary to start the work and requires practice. As I mentioned, you can start with the most basic things you already have; what is important is that you learn how to speak the language of cinema.

<< 3 >>

Where to start?

You may have already done some work in this field. You may have done some short films but feel they didn't come out right. You should not lose sight of your inability and say this work is hard and impossible, on the contrary it is very simple, just needs a bit of patience and focus. Most importantly, remember that the main thing in your work is continuity and practice. Although not necessary for now but knowing a series of cinematic terms is useful. I also try to share my experience with you in simple language and if necessary I will explain these terms as well. You can acquire tutorial books and get acquainted with the classical concepts of cinema. But I recommend that you don't go for other books in the next few weeks as we will experience many things together here. After a while, you will be drawn to these books to overcome your needs.

Do not worry about learning cinematic techniques. Gradually, through making films and maybe taking some short courses you will get familiar with them. So now we take our camera and start filming without any background. We can start with ourselves. You know yourself better than anyone else. Most definitely you will be the only viewer of this film and after watching it you can either keep it or delete it. Clearly you do not have to answer to anyone since you are independent from the beginning. So don't be afraid, put the camera in front of you and criticize yourself with courage. Talk about your good and bad qualities, confess, and say whatever you want. Now watch your film and see if you are the person you really are in front of your own camera. You'll better understand how outspoken you have been about the facts and insights of yourself, or how much you have been lying to yourself, and have gotten far from reality. If everything is true, you should be happy because you learn to tell the facts from the very beginning. Although not comfortable but this will be your first positive step in the process of filmmaking.

You are going to be a filmmaker with your own unique features since the same character will be reflected in your movies. If you fabricate somewhere in the movie, you will hate yourself later when reviewing it. So you will never lie to your audience. When you are filming behind the camera, you will be honest with your audience and this will make them commit to your films with complete confidence and trust. It may be hard at first to confess everything in front of the camera. But no problem, wait for a few days. During these days you will struggle with yourself a lot. You will try to rethink your behavior and make yourself ready to go in front of the camera again. So push aside your bad behaviors and enhance your good qualities. Days will pass and then you will be ready to sit back in front of your camera again, you will see how different the film is compared to the first one. This is a self-made practice. It's a great step to have made such changes and become honest with yourself over few days. Know yourself well enough first in order to make your surrounding environment understandable to others. This is a self-made practice. You can also do this with people close to you. Put them in front of your camera and assure them no one will see it without their consent. Then leave them alone and let them say whatever or as much as they feel like in the front of the camera. Then show the movie to them only. They usually have no problem with you watching it if you get their permission first. You certainly notice what special and distinct moments can be captured. Your camera is the medium between them and their personal reality. Expressing the facts is also pleasing to them. Your camera will become your secret box and comrade of all pains and it will even become habit to sit in front of it every day and pour your heart out. In the same way, you need to make your camera create the same sense for the people you work with. That is how you can gain their trust to sit in front of your camera. You have to do these practices regularly to get to know yourself better and to get rid of your weakness and to make your camera an inseparable part of your existence.

Your camera should be at the service of your subject. Later on these practices make your camera unnoticeable. The subject itself will tell you what to do with it. For many of those technical people the camera becomes noticeable because they are so concerned with the techniques that they ignore what is happening in front of the camera. Technique is good if you use it in right situations, but likely it will spoil the film, confuses the viewer and takes away the main objective if it's not used correctly. Audience sees your world through your camera and it's your duty to show them a clear cut world as much as you can. You might say that audience is none of your concern when personal enjoyment is the purpose of your work, but keep in mind that you are the first and the best audience for your own movie. So for that sake make the best.

<< 4 >>

First Steps

When we start any light or heavy exercise we need to warm up first to prevent any possible damage. To begin filming, we also need to work out to get prepared. It is true most of this work is based on our creativity but it should not be forgotten that practice is essential for acquiring physical skills.

What's the difference between a skilled hunter and a beginner? A skilled hunter, apart from having an eagle eye, knows the timing and possesses quick action and is less likely to go into error, why? The answer is clear; he knows both the prey and the hunting-ground. He knows when the prey appears. He knows its hiding places. He knows where to set up the gear to have a best view at the prey. These are all the characteristics of a skilled hunter who has been practicing over and over. He has certainly practiced shooting at dummy targets and wasted many rounds left and right to make his aim better and better.

Now let's assume we are that hunter, our camera is the rifle and the subject as our prey. We naturally have to acquire the skills. A hunter is always known for carrying his gun on his shoulder, we should always have our camera with us too, even if we are not supposed to shot anything. In that case, if suddenly something happens unpredictably in front of our eyes we won't feel guilty of not having the camera to record it.

Like the hunter we must have an eagle eye and strengthen our aiming.

So start filming from any interesting thing that catches your eye at any opportunity. It doesn't matter what you are filming. What's important is to get used to the camera viewfinder. You should get used to be like a camera lens. Your eyes will get used to seeing an image in open or closed view. You grasp different lens properties and recognize which lens or shots work best with your subject by looking in the viewfinder a lot. As you know, the focal length of our eyes is the same as a normal lens. We slowly learn from camera lenses how to see things without a camera in wide or Tele view (open or closed view). Our eyes slowly get used to this kind of seeing. We need to be able to quickly set ourselves at the best place to have more control over the subject, and we do not have to change our angles to get the best shot. These practices should be done every day. Many times we can do these practices without the camera and with our eyes only. We need to choose the best place to sit and see the surrounding, from a taxi to a coffee shop, at parties or in a stadium watching a soccer match.

We need to learn to control our shaky hands so that the hunt is error free. Most events are unrepeatable and we may lose the chance if we are not in full control of ourselves or the camera. You've probably seen it many times that a captivating subject get lost and wasted by negligent filming, which unfortunately will not be repeated. It only takes practice to make the right decision and not to miss anything. To do this, try filming social events as much as possible to get smooth hands.

It's obvious you have to focus when you have the camera in hand and looking through the viewfinder to capture a scene. But at the same time this will make you overlook what's happening around you, and in many cases especially in times of crisis this can be risky. In these cases, the sense of self-protection will unconsciously make you react to the surrounding danger which may destroy your concentration and damage your rushes. In such cases, you should learn how to have indirect look while focusing on your main subject; to keep an eye out all around. If you do have an assistant let them be on the watch.

At the start of your work, events taking place in front of you are usually so attractive that you spend all your time filming them, but when you go for editing you feel something is lost or you have nothing. The thing is that you should not ignore the reactions around your subject. One reason you don't shoot from surrounding subject is that you don't want to lose the main subject. So you have two solutions, have a second camera to film the reactions around you or secondly, spend time and get enough film from the main subject, then find and film the appropriate reactions around the subject. If possible you may try to rebuild the reactions which of course will be a bit difficult. So the best way is having a second camera. If you're working alone, you can quickly and safely fix the first camera and turn it on to capture the main subject and use your second camera to film the reactions. The difficulty starts when you are alone and encounter documentary or unrepeatable scenes. But the story is completely different for the scenes that can be replicated. You can capture these scenes with peace of mind and then film the responses of surrounding people.

For scenes like demonstrations and street clashes you can take the camera high up. Or level it with your eyes in front of your face for better control. This way it won't be necessary to constantly look at the camera's viewfinder.

If you don't want to miss surrounding reactions then move your eyes around and quickly rotate the camera to that direction. To get the skill for capturing such scenes it's best to practice beforehand. One best way is filming a football match. This way you will be skilled in filming unpredictable scenes by using the camera on your hands. Your fear of the camera will die out with practice and it will no longer be cumbersome. This way it will be just a device for recording events that are happening in front of your eyes.

One of the problems most novices face is the lack of timely detection for filming. Although they carry camera with them at all times but are less likely to use it. Their excuse is always that they did not have a good subject to take. The reality is something else. They expect to see beyond what is in front of their eyes so they easily miss the usual things they see every day. I must say there is no need for a strange thing to happen to become your subject matter. Everything has its own routine and it's you who have to see the world around you in different way. You need to change your perspective as everything is so attractive and fresh. When you wake up and want to go out, know the angles, the views and what to expect for that special hunt. It is clear nothing will happen if you walk the same path with the same glances every day without that searcher eye.

So when you go out for a walk, target a specific subject and focus on it or whatever that is related to it. For example, one day let the birds in a crowded urban environment to be your subject. You will notice right away that the first thing you see exiting the house is the first bird that comes along, your camera automatically turns to it. You will be looking up and down the sky more often or over the heights of the buildings or the electrical beams. You will see angles that never caught your eye before. That is how everything will be new and you constantly discover things. The reason is that you look at the surrounding with a new perspective.

Imagine this, a bird is caught on the electrical wires and a pedestrian is trying hard to call the firefighters to come and save it. Time goes by until firefighters come and rescue the bird. Meanwhile, a school girl stands and watches the whole scenes. You can create a film about every single moments of this scenario, and the subject is the bird at all time. You see what we gained when we outlined the subject and turned our head up to see the bird? Perhaps, if you didn't target the bird as your subject it would never be noticed and your eyes would look straight ahead just like any other day and miss the subject.

<< 5 >>

First ideas

Now let see how ideas form in our mind and where do they come from. Do you have to sit at home and write something based on your imagination to make a film from it? In that case, are you sure you will portray these fictional stories one day at all? Do you have the budget and the facilities to do it? Many students in this field or most novice filmmakers go for ideas that cost too much to make. They wait for many years and do nothing else, and finally due to no results they turn away disappointed and leave the job. We need to be realistic about the events around us and make the best use of our limited facilities. We have to move in order to get something. We find different issues in our surroundings during daily searches. Our curiosity makes it easy to focus on those topics, and we begin to focus and slowly grasp different angles and finally dominate it. That is how our imagination helps us form stories. It's best to work on subjects you master. Those who are familiar with their subject matter and live with it are usually more successful in making a movie from it. Once more, I must remind you the films you are making are not intended to be seen by anyone except you, and you should look at them as personal experiences which are only for practice. You do realize that the cinema which is based on large capital is not what we are looking for here. We are making a promise to ourselves to make our films with the least amount of possibilities and budget. However, you never know, the same films may become your best films. So without any anxiety do whatever you like in them. Add and cut. Repeat filming over and over until you get the desired result. If you don't like then delete it. Do not worry, no one is looking over your shoulder and you don't have to answer to anyone. Remember you are working for your own enjoyment.

Try to choose topics you know and are sure have the ability to make it and do not have to pay for it. Scenarios are all around us and you don't need to go far to find them.

To begin with, we should not go into issues that require licensing from some organization. Dealing with such issues, apart from wasting your time in the pre-production period and restricting you, will generally cause obligations that will deprive freedom of action. So, the best thing to do at the moment is simpler issues that don't involve these problems. Don't insist on troublesome issues.

Open your eyes to keep track of subjects that have surrounded you for many years, and be aware of stunning things that have the potential. You have upper hands on subjects and can easily capture them.

Your mind is activated by searching and many ideas

can form, although many of them are fleeting. Many of them don't have the capacity to become a film. Perhaps only one or more ideas can work. You can write down all your ideas and categorize them and select the most suitable ones at the right time.

Keep in mind that same ideas can simultaneously form in the minds of other people too. These ideas are general and everyone can think of it at first glance. You need to pay more attention to details and give life to your own stuff; topics that are not repetitive. This is relative to your point of view. For example, the issue of industrial wastes destroying rivers and causing disease and contamination and killing fishes is a general issue. For sure many others have thought about the same issue. So let this be your main topic but you create an entirely new, interesting and different issue from it; like a family living along the river and their everyday life depending on it, and how the pollution can change and affect their lives.

<< 6 >>

Do not forget to research

Our method is direct observation. So at first, we make direct observation without relying on research or books from previous people on the subject we are interested on. Next, we begin to study the subject in order to complete our information. We should also study any material relative to our subject as much as possible. Naturally, we will not use many of these researches in our film, but it will raise our understanding of the subject and make it more dominant. Then we start our work with full confidence.

My advice is to base your work on documentary films. Then if you like and the theme allows, add more story to it. You need to experience this kind of cinema to find your own way. Here, we don't intend to divide the cinema into a documentary or fictional; we are looking for something in between. You may choose to call it whatever you like. Our subjects are documentary and real. Subjects with such characteristics usually have a story in their belly, which can approach the storytelling cinema during the course of making and depending on our arrangement. We need to create a new and different work of cinematic expression through our own innovations. In the end, we will find and reach our own unique cinema as personal art. This will be achieved only if we are fully in control of our subject, and consider research as the main pillar of our work. The research considered here is not limited to field and classical, sometimes we need to sit and look at a sunflower field for hours to explore the mysteries of nature. The pleasure of this beauty is sometimes so great that you must make your camera a medium between you and the scenery and share it with others by recording it.

<< 7 >>

Use your own personal experiences

Extract your stories from your personal experiences. Usually filmmakers who use their own experiences make brilliant work. They rebuild their childhood memories and experiences, and since they are familiar with that space they can create an attractive and believable atmosphere that sits on the audience's heart. A number of them may display memories of war time or front line battles on the screen or others with sweet memories of their honeymoon trips. But here we are not going to restructure the past and build a cinematic film based upon it; we want to make films out of present. We don't want to bear the cost of rebuilding the past scenes, unless we already have the past images ready and want to combine them with the present. Here we are using our current experiences in film making. For the start you can choose a theme that you as a narrator will be the main character both in front and behind the camera. You may film your ongoing experiences, like climbing a mountain or a short family trip or perhaps a birthday party of a relative, or other similar events. Choose a simple and accessible theme and start filming, then edit and finish it.

Our current experiences are the things we are involved in and have control over; it can be sitting next to a fountain and enjoying the clear running water. In general, anything we spend time on and enjoy every day is considered our personal experiences. Many bitter or sweet things happen throughout the day but you cannot capture them all. When you intend to film your daily routines try to choose the most interesting one. This selection phase is very important, and bit by bit, by gaining experience and continuity in your daily practice you come to know which part of your daily routine is best for filming; this is the most important part of your filmmaking process.

With monopods that are now available to general public and are usually used for cell phone selfies, you can have fun with the making movies of yourself or a self-made-portrait. Some professional filmmakers have created selfie films with the same monopods and cell phones. This way, the person takes a film from himself and takes the story further. So you can get one of these monopods and become creative with it, try to shoot bits and pieces of your daily life and create stories based on it. Note that it is not necessary to use monopods all the time or only at you. It can be a combination of forward views from your own point of view or selfies using the monopods.

<< 8 >>

Is there a need for a screenplay?

The screenplay or scenario is the primary and main element of any movie that the film is based on. The screenplay is like the map that the film goes by it step by step. In professional cinema which is based on the precise planning of production and cost, it's hard to make movies without having a script. Producers are not often willing to make films without accurate and precise screenplay. But this story differs in some way for artistic and independent cinema because these producers know well they are dealing with filmmakers who usually violate the rules of cinema and are always experiencing and innovating. Many times the independent filmmakers begin with only a few pages of abstract story and complete it as they go on. These filmmakers know their work well and love to get into unpredictable situations and coordinate themselves. Of course, only a limited number of filmmakers are currently working like this. Many of them already have full proof screenplay, but according to the circumstances and the events that usually happen on the stage they are able to adapt themselves to new conditions and change the script on the basis of those events. That is, although maintaining the original framework of script, they give it a new form. There have been many films in the market without any script; they are slowly and consistently captured during filming.

There is no need for a specific script in the kind of film-making approach we discuss here. You can take notes, but my advice is to educate yourself to keep and save the beginning, the ending and sequences of you film all in your mind. Naturally this is a bit hard at first, but eventually it can easily be done by focusing on the main subject and not thinking about anything else. When we don't write details, we don't limit ourselves to film every bit and will be much easier to change or remove conditions. In fact, we are writing with our camera. When we make a promise to ourselves from the very beginning to film without written words and just flow with the camera and to depict what we want then we become accustomed to having a cinematic mind. Cinema is your art and the camera is the medium between you and the audience, not your pen. That is why the literary descriptions you usually read in novels do not have any place or value in the cinematic scripts and each sentence should be written in such a way that the equivalent can be pictured on the screen. For many years the debate has been as either the script has literary value or not? The script is written in order to make a film based on it and has no value by itself. Although there have been many screenplays that became valuable piece of history over time without turning into movies due to variety of reasons. But basically nobody writes scripts only to be printed; they write it to become a movie. Many screenplays published and made available to public were written from or after the movie was made and shown to public, in other words they are film-written, either due to lack of written screenplay or the script was subjected to so many changes during making. No matter how much the movie is already made in your mind based on the sights, people and the available space, the moment camera starts rolling and the first shot is captured everything changes and rest of your movie flows with the first scene. Therefore you should be ready to change your mind on the basis of new things, but at the same time keep the framework as what you already thought of before.

When we say we can begin filming without a script that doesn't mean we shouldn't have one, rather the main framework and everything we thought before is already made up in our mind. The difference here is that it didn't go on paper and we didn't limit ourselves to previous writings. This is one practice that makes your mind dynamic and you can distant yourself from literature and learn better cinematic language. Later on if you choose filmmaking as your main profession things will differ somewhat. Most definitely you will make movies with consistent and accurate scripts too. Even your experimental films will have solid scripts. These practices make your mind cinematic and learn the language from the beginning so if you were to write a script in the future you know how to do it well. Thus your screenplay will be a script that can be turned cinematically into a picture.

<< 9 >>

Do not doubt yourself

We'll never try and gain experience if we are constantly in doubt as whether this or that is right or wrong. First of all we must learn how to have independent personality and consequently independent decision making. If we are willing to do something from the bottom of our heart and believe we should do it right, we still have not lost anything even though we conclude later that we took the wrong path, so consider it as a new experience which is a good thing. But let's remind ourselves not to repeat experiences that already had negative results; following them is destructive and do not fit into our design.

Everything is done by trial and error. You will not miss anything by failing; rather you'll be more prepared for the next experience. But this won't happen if you put things off and don't get up and start working. I know many people who constantly talk about making a short film, talk about it to dozens of people and defiantly receive many opinions, but still to this day they have not taken a single step; they keep getting farther and farther from making it. These people are constantly in doubt if their plan is good or not. As a rule, they will never dare to experience. I don't say consultation with others isn't good, rather it's very useful, but remember it isn't necessary for your friends or colleagues to read and know your ideas. You will get skeptical when you hear their comments and suggestions and your decision making will become even more difficult. It's better to make your movie first, then ask their opinion about it. Suppose your movie isn't what you already had in mind, that's no problem. You should be happy to find your faults by filming. What's important is that you've gained the experience and made a film about your idea. Moving and gaining experience is better than sitting and doing nothing. You achieve unique knowledge only through continuous work. Only through this knowledge you can better understand the world around you and take joy in it. Only this way you can depict the beauty of the surrounding and share it with others through your art.

Any kind of doubtfulness prevents you from taking the path. Fear of failure makes you lazy and inactive. The main prerequisite in film business is the courage to gain new experiences.

<< 10 >>

Do not express everything together

Try to focus on just one topic. Express your subject simple and easy, don't make it complicated. You are not supposed to convey all your knowledge in one movie. The novice often wants to jam all the information they have on different fields in one film with any excuse they get. This will result in a meaningless and intolerable film. Viewers like to follow a single subject and they leave you as soon as you give them too much information. Leave the final word and decisions to the viewers and critics. Do not try to conclude your movies all the time.

Do not worry if you cannot express all your concerns in just one movie. Remember this is not supposed to be your last. So persevere your knowledge and take advantage of the subject in other films. Choose a simple subject and express it simple. Keep in mind that complicated topics can also be expressed simply. Do not distract yourself and focus on the main subject. Audience get confused by too many subjects and the opportunity to concentrate on the main subject will be lost. You need to skillfully pass on the information and then leave it to the audience to decide on whatever you are trying to express. You must make the audience to think. They feel good and watch your film more eagerly when you respect their intelligence. The magic of picture entice the audience in many ways. They may see and discover things that not even you knew about it. This is the power and characteristic of cinema.

To get started, make a short film with a simple story with one main character and possibly limited number of sub-characters. You are free to create new characters. Write dialogues for them and take them to you imaginative spaces and create imaginative stories for them. But my suggestion for the start is that you use actual and available characters around you. Let them live their lives and portray them naturally in front of your camera. They should have their own dialogues and use their own slogans. Their living environment should be real, and no need for you to design a stage for it. Their clothes are the ones they wear. Each one of them simply has separate life you can capture without slightest manipulation. The lives of these characters can later be a source of inspiration for longer and more professional films since you have seen their true characters and will certainly be more successful in portraying your story.

Some people start to phrase and jabber as soon as they get the chance. Such characters soon lose their admiration amongst people and since they make no sense no one give them value. Many filmmakers are the same and when the opportunity and possibility of filmmaking arises they want to use everything they possess in their film. This will result in amalgam of all the things they imagined as a masterpiece. If the time comes for you to experience a new film remember it won't be your last and you'll be filming over and over again. You will definitely have the opportunity to portray your ideas as time goes by. So put all your effort and focus on one topic and put away others to get better results.

You may include lots of ideas in your movie, but they all have to be directly or indirectly related to the main subject matter or complement necessary and relative information. Those with occupied mind can never finish a movie because they are hasty and want to picture every idea quickly. Various topics constantly flood their mind; this makes them leave the work unfinished and start another one and the next and next... The result is bunch of movies that have no ending. You can bring all your ideas into life in the right way if you are a bit more patient and focused.

<< 11 >>

Spend more time on editing

Editing is the most important part of your creativity. Your film must be solid enough so nothing needs to be removed or added. That's why you have to spend more time on editing. Even if your movie only contains a single shot you still have to think about possible editing. You must consider according to your subject matter if the shot should start in black or white, or if the title comes on black or colored terrain. All of these must be taken in to account in view of the subject matter. You have thought about it carefully and examined the psychological effects in advance.

Your editing method has direct relationship with your personality. If you are talkative, your film will definitely include extra shots filled with lots of talk. On the other hand, if you're a quiet person the same feature will have a direct impact on your movie. You may want to edit the film with small shots; of course this is not a general rule and does not apply to all, personally I take sense of humor with this group of beginners. Think about editing while shooting your film. After making few movies over time you'll be able to foresee your pre-edited film and know how approximate the shots should be during filming, or whether which shot is to be placed before or after the other. Of course, this only applies to movies that you have control over, not for documentaries when events are unpredictable.

Editing is the final stage of directing your film which is also the most important part. This requires that you have made the technical composition of the film (decoupage) carefully and have taken different and enough shots in order to edit with open hands and back and forth the shots until the logical story are achieved. The more time you spend on editing the better to outcome of your work. Every time the editing in done, copy it and watch it on TV or, or preferably on the screen to easily notice the faults. You may also give yourself a few days off and see your movie again; this way your sensitivity on favorite shots diminishes and you can better understand your mistakes. You can remove or shorten some scenes as needed and it will no longer be hard to dump them, the job will be much easier.

It is a good idea to think about editing while filming and know what you'll need later on so you don't leave out anything. Presume you will no longer return to the place of filming and need to complete the work right there and when. If you have enough time take some extra shots that you think will be useful when editing. In that case you will have enough choices for editing.

You need to learn some editing software so you can do it on your own. Editors in the professional industry have an important role in creating the rhythm and logical continuity of the film and are professionally specialized. This task is usually done by someone other than the director. But here you have to do both so you can experience the process of filmmaking from the beginning to the end. Your mistake will stand out when editing. You'll probably have to repeat some scenes or re-capture them again. This will result in thinking about editing while making your next film at the time of filming so you do not have to re-shoot the ones you need.

If you have formed a small filmmaking group and have divided the tasks among them, it is better for your editor to be present as much as possible while filming and take advantage of his consultations. If you have an editor, try to edit the shots taken on the same day, so if you needed more shots or had to re-capture any one of them you will have enough time to do it. Editors who edit movies can instantly make good and useful suggestions.

<< 12 >>

Cinematic time and real time

Naturally, the passage of time in cinema is different than normal life. Although there are instances when same amount of actual time is filmed but this is only under specific purposes. A regular example goes like this: your alarm clock rings, you get up from bed, take a shower, eat breakfast, get ready to go to work; all of this may take about an hour or less in real life. But if we want to show the same events in the cinema it should not take more than a minute. Of course, we should make the audience believe that one hour is passed. To do this, you need to observe few points so you can use at time of editing in order to create the sense of passage of time. The filming can start from the time the alarm rings and a hand enters the frame and turns it off. The next shot can be a view of the shower and the main character standing under the water. We can cut the shot here and go to drying the hair and face with towel, and then a shot of eating breakfast and the next plan inside the car or public transportation going to work. You see how we could reduce one hour of real life to a minute or less of filming with only four to five shots, each of which lasted between five to ten seconds? You can learn tricks of the trade by watching various films and learn the techniques used in their decoupage for inducing time in movies. Of course, you will later experience better ways in your own films.

In classical cinema, the visual effects such as blurring the image in black (fade out), in white (fade in), blending two images (dissolving), and other effects are used to simulate longer times such as day to night or vice versa. In today's editing many use less traditional techniques and usually cut the clip going from night to day, or past to future. Viewers have become accustomed to this kind of editing which are believable. The contemporary audiences have seen so many different films with unusual editing techniques that can easily see and understand new and innovative ways of editing and technical innovation in films that are intended for new experiences.

You do not have to wait to find a subject to practice various methods of simulating time; you can capture your daily routines and edit them for partial understanding of these techniques. Try to decoupage your daily activities such as eating breakfast, making lunch or dinner or going to the park and walking along with the least scenes, and reducing the duration of these activities to a minimum cinematic time.

<< 13 >>

Create the movie in your mind

You can create an image of the movie in your mind if you are well in control of the subject. Sometimes you know the starting point but not the ending, or vice versa. If your subject is kinds that you don't want to miss the time to make it then don't hurry and predominate it. Know the start and the end of your movie and know what it's supposed to be filmed. Do not worry about your time. You do not need to work on your movie theme day and night. Just do your daily routine and surely you'll get focused at any opportunity. This will gradually become a habit and fun.

It might have happened that you are making the film while dreaming in sleep. This is a good indication that your mind is involved with your movie. In fact, you are getting ready to make it. You create your film over and over in your mind and prepare yourself to start. This practice strengthens your mind and since it doesn't cost anything you may do it over and over again and each time develop it until the actual time comes to start filming.

<< 14 >>

Narrate the present time

Living in the past and wandering in the future keep you away from enjoying the moments that are passing by fast. Many of us tend to portray the past rather than the future. One reason is that we have seen and experienced things rather than the future that is unknown. Addressing the past requires its reconstruction and it is difficult in many cases. You are living in the present and you are in control, so it is best to pay more attention to present time. Future people will see their past community through your movies real well.

Life is moving on, if we live in the moment, move and take the normal paths, see the surroundings well and try to take full advantage of the moments then we'll be able to record those moments well in our works and become the illustrator of our time.

We are going to use our camera to enjoy the moments through the cinema art by personal and self-taught methods. We are devoted to save the beautiful moments of life, firstly to enjoy it ourselves and then share it with others. So here we have nothing to do with the past and will not judge it, or predict the future, rather work like clock hands, moving in present. Our camera also needs to follow the same path. The time in cinema is always on present, even when you go past or future in movies, what we see is the narrative of the moment. This same technique goes for writing scripts, we only uses present verbs. For example, if part of our script is about the past, we cannot use verbs like, was, had, and ate. In fact, it should be of a simple present day and verbs, and uses verbs such as Goes, eats and…. To write a novel, you are free to use any kind of the verbs, but not in screenplay or script.

<< 15 >>

Know your living environment well

So many things are right in front of our eyes but we are unable to see them. We don't have to go far, only need to open our eyes to see the surrounding better.

Right observation is essential for filmmaking. You may have noticed that someone used a subject, then after watching it you said to yourself why didn't I use that subject? It was right in front of my eyes too?

Many interesting and fascinating topics are all around but you pass them indifferently every day. All it takes is to realize that whatever that's normal to you may be much more interesting to someone else only a few meters away.

It's a good idea to start from your own home or neighborhood. Remember people are curious to see things they haven't seen before, were unable to see or limitation didn't allow. Your home environment and its people will definitely appeal to them. You know your parents and other family members well and bringing them in front of camera is much easier than strangers. You know them better than anyone else and know their inner characteristics. You can definitely capture them better.

Have you strolled through your neighborhood streets? Do you know how many houses there are? Do you know the people? Do you know what kind of people live behind the doors and what different stories they have? How many of these people you already know and are in contact with? There are as many stories as there are people living in your neighborhood, and it will take a decade if you tend to capture one day of their lives. We should always start from few feet away; First, our own home, then the neighborhood, city or village. Filmmakers who make films in their native environments are usually more successful and audiences connect with them better. They know all the reveled and unrevealed angles of their environment and are naturally more successful in portraying it.

There are as many subjects for filmmaking as there are people living on the planet and each character has unique point of view. Each one views the universe differently. We need to work with these differences in filmmaking. These differences make up our stories. Suppose you are about to make a film about the people in your neighborhood. Choose a person from different levels, an old woman, an old man, a boy and a girl, a housewife, a vendor, a construction worker ... Now depict one day of each character life and their relationship with each other separately. Although the films are done in the same neighborhood but when comparing you will see all movies are completely different. That's because you filmed from their perspective. But if you wanted to interfere in the subjects then your films would all look similar.

It is no exaggeration to say we can dedicate our entire life filming our neighborhood and never repeat any subject. It would be much better to make movies from limited number of people around whom we know rather than complete strangers that have no knowledge of.

<< 16 >>

Be your own producer

Try to make your movie with the least amount of money as possible. If you find yourself in a situation that requires expense don't waste time looking for a producer because nobody is willing to pay for your personal experience. You should pay for your own experience. Do not nag that if you had the funds and the facilities you could have created a masterpiece. You must first gain plenty of experience and prove yourself by making low-cost films then find a producer for your future bigger films. So get on your feet as soon as possible and start working with available resources without relying on others. Don't put the guilt on others for your undoing. You are wrong if you sit home and wait for someone to appear and pay for your expense. You withhold the pleasure of filmmaking from yourself by sitting and doing nothing. Don't be afraid and start. That's how you find your weaknesses; by experiencing. You won't find food until you are hungry, and when you're hungry, you'll make a gourmet food from the simplest things available.

Producing in the cinema you started is much different than professional cinema. You are the producer of your own movies. But it doesn't mean you are going to use your own money. You have to take advantage of your facilities and available credit among people. Your financial constraints should not be a reason not to do your movie. You can certainly start and finish your work just with the help of your own pocket money. The advantage is that you won't be under the shadow of a producer and no one will look over your shoulder and can safely do whatever you like. Many professional film-makers wish they could return to their starting point to create their favorite film with complete independency and without the presence of movies producers, which includes all the limitations that goes with it. So take advantage of the opportunity and make most of the facilities available and enjoy to the fullest possible.

<< 17 >>

Actor's role

Remember that you were the only actor in your first movie as mentioned above? You showed up in front of the camera with that notion, no matter if you played as an actor or just as yourself. You appeared as your own character in the film.

People can play their own character better than anyone else because no two are the same. So if someone has to play your character who else better than you.

This also applies to others in your story and everyone should play their own character. Keep in mind that you are not working under usual conditions and methods of filmmaking. So you can use ordinary people playing their own character which will be more believable and easier to work with in front of the camera. When you bring out your story from streets and people's lives, the same characters which the story is based upon are best options to play the role and go in front of your camera. You do not need to tell them how to play; it's enough to say the movie is about their life and they should just be themselves.

Your task is to control the normality of people in front of the camera and to be careful they don't play a fake role. This depends on your correct guidance as the director. You have to use tricks that they can be comfortable and unobtrusive in front of the camera.

<< 18 >>

Do not overlook the possibilities of sound

Sound is fundamentally important in films. If an image gets corrupted somewhere in your film it can be offset by a good sound. But it will be almost irrecoverable if it is other way around. In the first step, you need to record the sounds as best as possible at the scene, and later on add extra sounds as needed at time of sounding. First, we work with the same microphone that usually comes with all cameras, provided we use standard distance between the source and the camera. I don't say don't use remote control microphones or professional voice recorders; my emphasis is not to stop your work due to lack of sound capabilities. The initial experiences will reveal your shortcomings later on when reviewing it. So, naturally you'll try to get more professional sound with better conditions in your next film. I know providing a good microphone will be costly and you still have to pay even if you rent one. But you can find friends who can lend you a microphone or save money bit by bit and purchase one you need to work for the next movies.

Sound and video are complementary. Most often the sounds coming from surrounding have much more effect than the image itself. In other words, it's much more cinematic. For example, the look on someone's face hearing the sound of a car crash or hearing the sound of a shotgun and the death of a soldier followed by the look on his partner's face. Some production costs can be avoided often with these tricks. Consider this: your main character is looking out of the window and we need to show people rushing to the street for demonstration. As a rule, we should show character's point of view looking at people rallying in the street. But making this scene is costly; therefore we can easily find a sample from the audio archive and add it to the look on character's face at the window to get the desired result. This example shows that many topics which you might think needs high budget or facility can be done with almost no cost at all. Now that you understand the importance of sound, keep in mind that if you were not able to capture an image, at least record the sound that will surely be useful in the future. You may even make a movie based on it.

<< 19 >>

Where is music in your work?

The most important use of music is helping to convey different emotions in the film. Music sometimes changes the normal sense of a scene. For example, a sad music played on a wedding scene with special purpose to transmit specific conception. Many famous movies are known for their music and without them, or if with see those along with some other music would totally lose their familiar charm. Flash tones that are only heard for few seconds are responsible to intensify situations and in many cases they have a warning role. For example, music can prepare us for some special event happening beforehand. Victory in a battle may be complemented by an epic music. Now, the question is can we use music in films that are less costly or no cost at all? If yes, then what kind of music do we use and where should we find it? Many don't like to use music in their films and only use it for the ending. Perhaps they suspect music deprives their images from being realistic. They have their own set of rules for using music. They do not use the soundtrack from outside the scene or use them suddenly. Instead, they say music must be heard from the scene itself to make sense, like hearing it from the car music player.

You can read many books on music tracks, but my suggestion for the starters is to keep your options open until you feel right what's good for your movie. The important thing is to enjoy it for now. You can use from huge collection available online. So don't limit yourselves and don't get swayed by other movies. Use music wherever you feel there is a need. If you have a friend or partner who knows music better than you ask for their help. You may also be specialized in music yourself, so make a suitable and fascinating music tailored to your film.

Listening to a particular music while making your own movie will greatly help to get the feel of the scene. You can define the length of your shot much easier by listening to specific music that is close to your plot. For example, you need faster beat music for stirring scenes with multiple shots. The start and end point of each beat can be inspirational for start and end of your shots.

<< 20 >>

How to determine the size of your shots?

The ways you choose the size of shots depends on the feeling you get form that scene. It is true that sequence of the different views are subject to certain rules, but we all know breaking the rules in cinema has never been a crime. Many filmmakers are interested in starting their scene with an open view, then get to the closed view bit by bit, or vice versa.

When you're in a scene, depending on your main topic and priorities, you need to listen to your feelings and start from there. You may take the whole scene in close or open views, that's no problem; it's your point of view. You have thought about these shots before and most of all, you like this method and enjoy it. So make your own stage. Decoupage or technical separation of the shots is different for each movie. Each scene decoupage is based on particular logic and also it would be a mistake to imitate from other films. If you know your subject and characters well then the scene will transfer the feel and you will unconsciously determine the size of the shots; they allow the viewer to more easily focus on the main subject and for you to transfer the message better.

It's hard to make movies when events are unpredictable. This will depend heavily on your skill and your quick decision to choose the size of the shot. You need to focus on the main subject and specify the size based on it. In such scenes, I try not to change the size of the shot without reason as far as I can, but if it is needed, I would do it at the right time, like when there is no dialogue or special action on the scene. That would when I don't have to cut off the scene. Otherwise I try to change the size of my shot by moving the camera. In such cases your work is much easier if you have a second camera. If you don't have someone to help you with the second camera you can set it in a fixed position to capture more general or specific view that reflects the responses to the original subject.

<< 21 >>

Select the right camera location

When you go to a stadium to watch a match you want to sit somewhere to have the best view in terms of playing field and both teams. Or when you go hunting, you have to be in a position to have a best view of the prey. In the same manner you need to be positioned to have a good view of your subject when filming. Choosing an inappropriate view angle will not only waste your time and money but also hurt your artistic work. When you don't carry a camera and don't intend to make a movie, try to look carefully at the places and find appropriate angles. You can avoid multiplicity of views by choosing the right angles. For example, if you are filming a communication between a salesperson and a customer at supermarket, there is no need to take consecutive shots from the salesperson or vice versa from the customer. Just bring the camera behind the sales counter and record a single shot from both.

You can select the best viewing angle in an open view. Suppose we want to shoot an entire sequence in one view, then the camera position and appropriate angle are very important. Choosing the right angle depends on many factors. If there is acting to be done in your scene, the camera's location should be selected according to their location, as well as necessary accessories like tables and chairs for the scene. Or if there is a vehicle in the scene, or a landscape view that has a great impact on your story, the camera location should also be based on their layout. There are no specific rules to determine the angle of the camera; it all depends on your feelings of the scene. Many directors choose the angle and camera location instinctively. Of course, this does not mean you should not decoupage the stage beforehand. Obviously, you've already seen the scene beforehand and have chosen the size of the shot given the feeling you got from the scene. By seeing different movies and analyzing them you can get a complete understanding of the matter.

<< 22 >>

Your eyes and ears make your cinema

Eagle's eye is sharper than any other bird because its nature is to hunt from the sky. That sharpness is the reason it gets the prey. We see with our eyes and hear with our ears. This kind of work requires you to have sharp eyes and good ears to hear the surrounding. You need to teach yourself to see the unseen and hear the inaudible. This quality is what makes you see and hear the surrounding. So your eyes and ears make up your cinema. But what do you see and hear that others are incapable of? The fact is that others also see and hear like you. They don't see or hear anything less than you, the only difference is in how. You should be more sensitive as a filmmaker. Ordinary people easily pass by many types of scenery, only have quick looks and details don't matter to them. But you have to learn not to pass by indifferently. Stop to see and hear. When you are in nature you may discover many things that ordinary people are unable to find. If others seek refuge in the nature for fun and entertainment, you have to go further for revelation and deliberation.

Have you ever met a detective? His job requires sharp eyes. He sees things around the crime scene that others are incapable of. He has two eyes and two ears just like all of us, but the difference is that he focuses more precisely on a specific subject and notices everything relevant to the subject matter which is the scene of committed crime. Therefore, he tries to recognize the relationship between the main and lateral story. We should focus all our senses on the main issue relative to our film like a detective. Every detective has his own way of discovering the truth and that is what makes him different from others. You also have to discover your unique ways to see and hear for your own cinema.

<< 23 >>

What is a good movie?

What criteria should we look for when choosing a good movie and basically who should identify and present a good movie? Have you ever wondered why the works of great sculptors like Michelangelo, Raphael, or paintings of Van Gogh or Dali, or music of Beethoven and... are undying? And why the works of many other artists in the same era didn't have the same fate?

The reason is simple and clear; those works were good, and good work continues to find its identity over time. It is the passage of time that distinguishes good and bad work. Genuine work always last. Genuine work has integrity and comes from the conscious mind of the artist. An artist who is well aware of himself, his environment and his community and the key to his work is honesty. So it is natural to create a work that reflects his inner self. His work cannot be bad and will surely last.

A good movie is a movie you see over and over again throughout your life, and enjoy it and discover new things every time you watch it. A good movie is a movie that you watch in your childhood, young age, old age, and every time you see it seems like the first time, and each time you perceive newer things.

These movies do not belong to their filmmakers anymore and will be among the spiritual assets of humanity and will be preserved for generations to come. These are the films that I call good. Many artworks may be unloved at the time of their creation and that depends on the historical period in which they were made. Many of them may have faced bad luck, the factors are many, but the passage of time has always determined their fate and true position. Some artists are ahead of their time and we need to wait until their art is appreciated. If our intellect doesn't allow us to understand their work now, it doesn't mean they are bad. They will be better known several decades later more likely and we change our mind about them. Good art is like a treasure that comes out of the ground as time passes.

<< 24 >>

Watch good movies over and over again

Watching movies is considered the best kind of class for filmmaking, but that doesn't mean you have to watch everything that has been made. You should see good movies over and over again. Many great filmmakers in the world have learned the cinema only by watching good movies repeatedly and this is recommended by most of them. The rules of cinema can gradually be learned by books or educational films that are available on virtual networks. The same books and educational videos will also refer you to movies of the cinematic history index from the beginning to the present. When watching in privacy, go back and forth on a particular scene repeatedly and examine its technical details and discover its hidden points. By watching several good films, you'll be aware of the main components of the movie and learn how to compare it with other movies. This way you learn all the commonly used formulas of filmmaking and notice the differences. The knowledge you gain this way will set in your mind automatically and when you want to make your own film in the future will help avoiding reproduction; something that do not resemble any other.

<< 25 >>

Find people like yourself

You will definitely receive positive or negative reactions from your audience by sharing your movie in virtual spaces or elsewhere. By doing so, you will be more closely connected to viewers and you will be able to see their films too. This will start your friendship with them. You should find friends and colleagues who love practicing and experiencing like you. In this case, you will understand the language well and you can share your experiences too. The continuation of these friendships may lead to mutual cooperation, which will be very positive since you won't be alone for your next movie, and if you are supposed to do a bigger work, you can count on their help and friendship. You may take part in their films with no expectation or wage, and they will also do the same for you. Ultimately, you'll be happy with the experiences gained.

However, my insistence here is to avoid using additional factors in your movie as much as possible. Try to make short films with minimal help and single-handedly. But keep in mind that cinema is a collective art in which number of professional elements in different disciplines together create the work. We must realize that each film in its place is an experience for its maker; even apart from categorizing them as good, medium or bad.

<< 26 >>

Have a certain place to present your movie

You'll make two kinds of movies. The first categories are the movies you create only for yourself which come from your personal experiences. These movies are watched only by your and stay in your personal archive. The second categories are the ones to be distributed among people to see. So you have to think about different and suitable places to present them. You can test your luck and send your movie to different TV channels. But remember these networks have their own standards and goals in terms of both subject and quality. You may have to wait a long time and still your movie will never be played. So don't rely on these networks alone and try your luck elsewhere. If your movie is attractive and engaging enough, it's possible that those networks will find you and want to purchase and broadcast your movies.

Virtual networks are best places for your movie to be released. You can use or create private network places such as YouTube, telegrams or similar sites with the smallest cost to show your films and increase your members through trick of the trades every day. Of course, if your movie has the potential to be presented globally, it's best to take it to a professional distributing company. This will not cost you anything at first but a share of your film's revenues which is usually about thirty percent of its profit is common. Of course, these companies may charge you for shipping and relative costs of paper work which will be insignificant. It is in your best interest to bare these cost so you can spend your time more on creating movies.

Other places where you can show your film are the universities. Different universities around the world have a section on films in their archive for students in various fields. Representatives of these universities each year buy films in number; fiction, documentaries..., and while showing the movies, the Filmmakers are also invited to analyze the films with the presence of experts and students during the screening and critique sessions.

Charity foundations, various ministries, educational institutions, airlines and public transportation and ... are places where you can negotiate and present your films.

<< 27 >>

Avoid moving camera unduly

Each camera movement has its own psychological impact on the viewer. Those who hold a camera for the first time get excited and turn it to any direction or zoom in or out with no purpose. But eventually the thrill subsides over time and the movements get calm. Moving the camera in cinema has its own rules and is subject to situations that arise with the scene. To get started, try to fix the camera. I recommend a tripod that you can handle horizontal and vertical (pan and tilt) movements smoothly. Try not to hold your camera on hand as much as possible. Many of those who just start filming think holding the camera by hand make their film more realistic. We see most of them not using tripod or other means and take their whole film with the camera on hand; unfortunately they do not give anything to the audience except headache and dizziness.

The camera-on-hand technique may be good for news documentaries, especially footages from battle grounds when there is no time or security to set up a tripod.

Later, filmmakers who wanted their film to come

closer to reality and documentaries used the on hand technique to imitate those films. Of course, I don't mean you shouldn't use the camera on hand technique in any way, rather my point is that logical and accustomed use of this technique can in some cases help the structure of your films. For example, holding the camera on hand is probably the best way for street conflicts when the whole scene has to be in one shot. This is definitely both acceptable and tolerant and will have good impact on the audience.

There is no specific rule for moving the camera. This depends entirely on your scene and the action and reactions within the scene and the rhythm of your work. It may also depend on the mood and style of the director. We need to understand that basically the movement is what distinguishes the cinema from any other art of photography. The two simple moves of Pan and Tilt (horizontal or vertical) motion have the most use in movies. Sometimes the combination of these two and the measured usage can change the structure of your movie and its rhythm. With these simple moves we can often delete extra verbal explanations and cut the time. In fact, your movie structure will approach the cinema language. For example, in a scene with horizontal movement (Pan) you can move the camera from boxing match photos hanging on the wall, then take it to the shelves where the championship medals are arranged, and then a vertical movement (tilt) going to the bed where a man with wounded face is laying on it. This movement without any written text or verbal explanation tells the viewer that here is the room of a boxing hero who is the main character of the film.

To move your camera, everything depends on story type and the way you make your movie. In a romantic film that is based on sentimentality of the main characters and where the music is the main component, you have to use different moves. For example, you have seen many times that the father and the son hug each other after being far apart for years, simultaneously the soundtrack intensifies their inner state. Naturally the camera won't have its full impact if it is fixed and it should move around them. You'll see the psychological impact and feel the moment. Or, for a police chasing scene, whether or not we are forced to have camera movement due to the nature of these movies. It is natural these movements require special equipment and of course with the relative expenses and other special factors involved. At the start of our work and considering the kind of cinema we're working on we need to approach these with caution. We must disregard them as much as possible and take other measures. We should try our best to take advantage of two simple but functional features; horizontal motion - pan - and vertical motion – tilt- of the camera. Many successful films around the world have been made by fixed-motion camera. This does not mean their rhythm is slow. Incidentally, fast-paced movies with fast rhythms are mostly done by editing.

Of course it would be a completely different story if you decide to become a professional filmmaker having the conditions and resources to make such movies in the future. Then your hands are open to decide your technical composition of views with less financial concern. In either case, remember that the story and logical transitions of the implied concepts are superior to technical issues. You should never sacrifice your story for technical playacts. I know it's tempting to use advanced equipment for your movie but let the story itself tell you what to do. If you see just one tripod is enough for the whole movie then do it. You should not be tempted to sacrifice your film for technical desires even if you have a truck load of different gears and equipment.

If you are really interested in movements, or your subject is such that you must use various movements, I suggest using new cameras that are available in market with same price as a cell phone. You can take good movement shots with these cameras without the slightest slip. These cameras provide super-awesome images without the slightest slip due to an ultra-slim stabilizer in them. One of them even has a suitable microphone built in it. Just go to the internet to see and select different types.

Simple and inexpensive lighting

One of the features of digital cameras is the ability to film in low light with the least lighting options available both for indoor and outdoor scenes. That is why those heavy, expensive and old lighting equipment used for negative films has been replaced with new, cheap, and lightweight equipment's that make the lighting easily and quickly.

As a general rule, the purpose or basis of internal and external lighting is to imitate and strengthen the natural light available in the scene. Meanwhile, lighting at night is far more difficult and time consuming. Let's start with a simpler example. Let's consider a room with a window, at night, and our light sources are the moonlight that shines through the window and also a night lamp or even a candle. Naturally, for the lighting of this scene, our main lights are moonlight through the window and the candle or the light of the bed side lamp. Sometimes the moonlight is so strong that with these full-frame digital cameras you don't need to amplify the light with synthetic bulbs. You can shoot with available light, but if possible it's best to use extra light for better image quality.

It's better to checkout your scene first. If you are going to a place for the first time and you're supposed to shoot at night try to boost the main source of lights available in the scene. For example, instead of a 100 watts bulb that are usually used at front doors, take a 300 watts bulbs and place them quickly. Once you finish your work, you can again remove the bulbs and use it for another scene. You can also have two or three small rechargeable and very lightweight spotlights. These spotlights rest on lightweight portable tripods which all can fit in trunk of your car. These lights will help you to make the depths at night by pointing them at certain places. As a rule for night lighting, look at the camera's viewfinder to see the light at the depth of the scene in black. This will create the depth of field necessary.

The most important thing to consider in lighting is the optimal use of existing source in the scene. For example, if we are going to go to someone's home for an interview, it's better to do it during the day to use the natural sunlight. If the house has a yard or garden we can interview there under sunlight. Otherwise, we need to look inside the house, room to room, to find a suitable place, or an open window to make use of the sunshine and interview the person there. On the other hand if we are to do the interview at night then we should have the person close to one or more light sources, like table lamp, or under the ceiling light or use our portable lights to shine on his face. Just remember to do all this quickly so the person doesn't get tired of the activities and do not deprive them of privacy or relaxing.

<< 29 >>

Costume and stage design

To give make better climate to our film we can replace, add or remove things with the fitting of the scene or possibly change the color of the doors or walls where we are supposed to film. The same goes for character's clothing and costume. We can ask to see their own clothes and choose the best among them in terms of color and design appropriate to the scene. In many villages, when people realize that they are supposed to be filmed they go and wear new clothes. The problem is that they go and wear city clothes, but we are looking for local costumes and we can ask them to wear their local clothing. It is a good idea to go to the desired place one or two days before filming and ask them to make the necessary changes to their decoration, so the space won't look artificial.

Costume design has a crucial and sensitive role in cinematic filming. Making and designing an environment for filming both in terms of time and expense is much more cost effective than filming in natural and real life.

For the beginning we are not supposed to bare a lot

of cost for costume or stage design. So, we will try our best to use available furniture or by rearrangement provide a more attractive scene. We can also choose from the clothes the main character brought by himself to have better coordination with the scene.

I also suggest you have several cans of different colored paint and a brush to paint a spot quickly if needed. But remember try to make the paint look a little bit old so it is not apparent you just painted it. However, I don't recommend making any changes to the scene as much as possible and let everything look natural and real. But if you must, it should be done so skillfully that it won't be apparent.

<< 30 >>

Know your strengths and weaknesses

You eventually begin to understand your weaknesses and strengths through work and practice. You need to work on your recognition so well that you can criticize yourself. This is done when you look at your work from third person's point of view. Try to be the first person to criticize your work. When you find the weaknesses try to correct them. I don't mean to redo the movie to make up for the mistakes. You should compensate for the weaknesses in your next movie to make it better than previous one. You need to be aware of your abilities and understand them. Try to strengthen and use them in the right instances to have stronger foundation. You will eventually find your abilities in one or more specific issues by gaining experience. That is when you need to concentrate on those abilities. By developing this ability, you will specialize in utilizing the best in your work. Take a paper and pen and write down your strengths and weaknesses. Then gradually begin to practice reinforcing both. You will gain a sense of self-confidence that is required to progress in your work by understanding your abilities.

<< 31 >>

Your subject should have the capacity to become a film

I already mentioned that capturing any subject is useful for your training, and by doing these practices you can prepare yourself for different experiences. Choosing the right theme for your movie is very important when you reach this stage. Not all topics have the capacity to become a movie and even If they do, they won't be attractive. There are many subjects that are suitable only for comedy and cannot be dramatic at all, and some issues are good for giving lessons. You need to be careful to choose a right subject that meets the criteria of cinema. I cannot clearly specify what subject is or isn't suitable to become a movie; this is acquired. You need to get it gradually by watching lots of movies. Of course, I am talking about movies that are created in the language of cinema; otherwise you see lots of movies that if you close your eyes and just hear the sound you still won't miss anything, they are more like a radio show. Our goal is not to make TV series or second grade commercial films. We are talking about a cinema that has a different language and separate from distasteful images made for fake entertainment.

Many of the pure ideas in cinema cannot be well defined. They just need to be created and to be enjoyed. Having cinematic sense and transferring it to the viewer is one of their features. This sense can neither be transferred by writing nor by explaining. You just have to see it. You need to get the insight on what is a good a subject to be filmed. It is your task to choose what subject is transmitted best to the audience. Sometimes a planned and well calculated scene will have such an effect and convey a message to the audience that nothing else has that transferring power. But this is done when the subject is rightly chosen from the beginning and has the capacity for cinematic language. Otherwise, it will not be worthwhile even if you shoot the most spectacular images with the best equipment. Many people use best lenses and technical equipment's for their films but the impact on the viewer is partial at the end because the subject didn't have the right capacity; the end result will not be desirable. On the other hand, having a nice cinematic idea may have great impact on the viewer even if it is done by a cell phone.

<< 32 >>

Have a workbook

As I already said, we should try to keep all ideas in our mind and not to write down anything because we strengthen our memory by doing so. But eventually the volume of our work expands and we need to record some important points so we don't forget them. Naturally, lots of information remains in our memory and when the time comes we gradually remember them. We only need to put down the key points so just at a glance can tell if we left out anything. Our mind is constantly developing new ideas and some of them will be useful in the future. It may become difficult to recall all of these ideas in the long run when they compile. So it's best to note and classify your ideas in a notebook to take advantage of them when the time comes.

Things that are not necessary to keep in mind are address and phone number of the people we are in contact with during production. A list of things needed for everyday filming and many other issues relative to our work should be written down. We may retrieve the workbook when really forgotten something, otherwise we have to be as dependent on our memory as much as possible.

<< 33 >>

Do not exhaust yourself

Do not waste your time on topics that ultimately lead to improper and inappropriate results. Sometimes we focus on topics that are only attractive to us. We may think we have discovered something important and don't even care about the advice of others, and since we feel our understanding is flawless we don't accept the truth and we insist on the subject that waste our time. Of course you are free to do whatever you like, but let's make the right choice. Sometimes it feels no matter how much you try you don't get anywhere. You feel something is missing, and whatever you do the result is unsatisfactory. Do not exhaust yourself. You have made an incorrect choice from the beginning. So don't insist on continuing and put your time and focus on another idea.

As I say don't try to grind the sawdust and learn from the experiences and recommendations of those who went the wrong way before you.

<< 34 >>

Go and travel

Travel makes you mature. The experiences gained through traveling will be very precious. You will be more focused and can take advantage of your time and opportunities that come along since no usual daily concerns are involved.

You may only focus on your films one or two hours a day on regular basis or due to daily routines, but you can concentrate around the clock when traveling. You can also take better advantage of your time if you travel alone.

Do not forget to take necessary and enough equipment with you. Devices such as extra battery or possibly a second camera is good not to miss out on something if the first camera breaks.

You always discover new things on the go and will try filming them. But don't get excited and confine yourself to these alone because later on you may find out they are incomplete, raw or just don't give out enough information.

So if you find something new and attractive try to spend more time on it and get familiar with the topic. Then start making a short film about it. You will have plenty of short films at the end of the journey that can either be watched alone or let others to see. You will definitely keep thinking about your observations along the way for a long time or may even find the theme of your next movie from experiences acquired.

<< 35 >>

Do not be afraid of new experiences

Art is trial and error. Useful and efficient results are obtained through these experiences. We will not be experienced enough if we don't put ourselves at test. Each failure will pave the way for more workable knowledge. You can use the experiences of others, but imitation and copying destroy the spirit of creativity. So do not be afraid to try new experiences. Cinema is not teachable; It must be learned by experience. To learn cinema you need to experience life in its various dimensions. Cinema is not everything; rather it is life as the essence that has to be experienced as best as possible. People learn the techniques but only use them to handle predetermined issues and as soon as something exceeds the usual formulas they cannot do anything. So they turn into technicians only to reassemble pre-made parts and they never create anything from scratch. Although we need to learn the techniques but that doesn't mean we have to specialize in every one of them. We can use other specialists to do our work. Our work is valuable only when all of it is genuine and not borrowed from somewhere else. We have to create and be creative and this can only be achieved by not avoiding new experiences.

Video Art, beyond expectation

Video art, as its name implies, has come to fore with the advent of video techniques commonly used by general public. People who have turned to this art are mostly artists from different fields of visual arts. Video art should not be compared with cinema or television. Looking at video art in a very common way, we may say it is just moving images sometimes accompanied by music with no certain meaning which is not even worth showing it to the public. But the fact is that video art like any other visual arts abstractly creates art that has a special place among its audience. Artists in this field have created amazing effects using digital cameras that can take hours of non-stop filming. Sometimes they take several hours of film from an old man lying on the bed while the camera is installed on the ceiling over him. Sometimes, on a faraway places, in the heart of the desert sands, or hours of film taken from a leaf falling from the tree in autumn winds. These artists can present their work anywhere, though television networks usually refuse to display these works to the public. But we sometimes see their works distributed on various occasions.

Animation and limitless imagination

The most enjoyable kind of filmmaking can be found in the world of animations due to creation of unimaginable scenes. Creating fantastic dreams and things that are far from reality, but still the most accurate scripts, decoupages and scenes, and in general whatever we expect from cinema can be found in such films. Animation is difficult, time-consuming and it takes lots of money and effort. As more than 200 technicians may work for over a period of nearly five years with huge budgets for a 90-minute animation. There has also been a huge evolution in the animation with the birth of the digital industry. Artists are now able to create magnificent effects at speed with wider possibilities that digital techniques can provide them. The digital industry in collaboration with technicians and artists gave the opportunity to filmmakers to combine animation with live films to create new stories such as animal friendship with people and stories like that. Stories we could not even think of before. All of these have come together to make cinema a masterpiece of humanity as the creator of amazing dreams.

We must admit that the main purpose of cinema

industry is to attract viewers. Most people want fun and attractive videos to be entertained for few hours. So the huge commercial industry must endure this need. As films get more eye-catching day by day, the expectations of the audience get even greater, and technicians in the field must think about new ways and solutions to attract spectators. That is why the production of imaginative films with animation techniques is one way of attracting audiences to cinemas.

Some of us are interested in creating animated films. The tools here are somewhat different and you must possess other abilities too. You can start making simple animations without a camera and gradually expand your work by using just a personal computer and a software program. You can create short animations single handedly and enjoy your work. It is best if you take some available training courses and learn the techniques well. Artists in this field must also have background in other visual arts such as drawing.

<< 38 >>

Don't make conclusions

We must leave the conclusion to the viewers and don't make any judgment ourselves. We find a lot of moral conclusions in the traumatic stories. The easiest thing to do is to have different conclusions in your movies. We must let the audience make their own impressions of the inner layers of our work. Let the end of your movie be open and not cling to ethical conclusions. It is tyranny if you want to have control over the viewers and enforce what's on your mind; naturally no viewers like this. Though cinema can be a good medium but there are other ways to convey moral messages. But we are here to enjoy the art of cinema and not obligated to finish our film with moral conclusions. If our goal is ethical we need to capture it in a cinematic format.

Remember that viewers have trusted you and given their time to get something out of it. You should respect their intelligence and finish your movie such that after seeing it they feel they gained some knowledge.

<< 39 >>

Don't waste your time on rubbish

Resist vulgar and tedious work. If you chose this job as your main profession and are now professionally engaged in making movies then try not to do any kind of work that comes your way. Have the power to choose. We learned here to be our own producer and not to work for anyone so we don't have to do whatever they wanted us to do. We need to be cautious if we are supposed to do this professionally. As the saying goes; don't leap before one looks. Pay attention to what you are going to do. First, research well and evaluate the aspects of the work, then do it. Do not worry if you don't have any work to do. If your work is good, be sure you won't stay empty handed. Movie environment is so small that you'll be pin pointed quickly and if you're not careful you will be rejected.

<< 40 >>

You are dealing with smart audience

Do not try to deceive your audience with handy tricks. They are clever; they have seen so many movies and are familiar with massive amount of information in the cyberspace that quickly know between truth and lie. There is a difference between making a film for our own satisfaction and making something for the public to see.

All it takes is to give few nonsense or unbiased things and then it will be difficult to get things back on the track. Cyberspace is so involved in movies that your production will be seen on the other side of the globe in the blink of an eye and then it will be out of your hands.

Naturally, you don't intend to do this. Ignorance, rush and not enough research may make you say irrelevant and unnecessary things. Remember you are not among your audience to explain or justify yourself. They will judge you based on the movie they see, not your writings about how or why you made it. If you want to deal with a common issue or take a public stand and your conclusion is based on it, then you need to be careful and put honesty as your first priority. Start and finish your movie in a way that nobody can object to it.

You have to act in such way that your work sets a motion so other people can complete it and follow your dream. Your films will be satisfactory if the conclusion isn't superficial and you haven't offended the audience's emotions, rather made them stand by you.

I say again not all your films are supposed to be like this. You are not making movies to save humanity. But if perhaps want the society to think twice about your film then you have to do it with special elegance. This kind of film making requires precision and expertise. You must acquire the knowledge. Learning the techniques alone isn't enough. You should research and study about the subject you are expressing well enough. It is to your best interest to take advantage of experiences from different experts relative to your film's subject and benefit from their consultation for your career advancements.

<< 41 >>

Have professional attitude

If you want to enjoy and be a professional in filmmaking, you must learn and stick to professional ethics and disciplines. When your film is done and presented to the viewer you need to obey the standards and respect their rights even if you have only a single spectator.

Every field of work has its own specific feeling and atmosphere. Filmmaking has its own rules too. People with different moods and spirits are involved in this field, but they have all one thing in common; they all love cinema. A painter sits and paints for hours alone and relaxed in calmness and silence. But filmmakers are obviously in contact with many people because this profession calls for it. So when it comes to our relationships with others we must adhere to social norms. Do not ignore the promises made or ethical "must" and "must not". Respect the rights of others and be accustomed to having professional ethics even if you work alone for your own personal desire. Being principled to ourselves and not imitating others is the kind of professional ethics that will benefit us firstly.

<< 42 >>

Don't waste time

When you start working, everything is fine and for a long time you are what you are. But the problem starts when you come upon things that can waste of your time. Watching your movie with others and possibly reviewing and criticizing it can be appealing and useful. It is worthy if you have the opportunity to do this for each of your movies. But you should not spend too much time on it. If you have a movie and feel it has the potential to be presented in various festivals then I think it's better to leave this job to people who specialize in distribution. There may be lots of disadvantages if you decide to do this yourself because it involves expertise and there are so many festivals in the world that will take lots of your time to find and participate in them and the temptation of traveling will not leave you alone.

One day you may open your eyes and notice you've spent couple of years at various festivals and have not made a single film during this time. Staying away from work isn't good. I know many people who participated in various festivals with their first film and didn't get the opportunity to make the second one for a few years afterward. They didn't even know how this happened.

Festivals are good places for other colleagues around the world to see your movies. It can also be a good market for your work. But you should not be dependent on them as they take your time. Winning or not winning a prize will be discouraging or overwhelming and all of these can delay your filmmaking progress and later on you'll come to regret the years lost. So put filmmaking as your first priority and always create new art.

<< 43 >>

Archiving and keeping movies

Your Films gradually pile up. Keeping and saving them is a must and has to be done carefully. Most movies are currently stored on the camera's hard drive but you must transfer them to another hard drive. Don't try overloading the drive and always leave one third of it empty so it won't slow down and also the sectors will not be damaged over time. Try to store your movies and information on two separate hard drives, so if accidentally one gets damaged or lost you have copies on the other one.

Over time, the volume of videos increase and you'll have trouble finding a specific image when needed. Categorize your videos and write profiles for each one and keep a list in a separate file from the beginning. Try to update the list at the end of the day so you don't have to spend a lot of time finding them. Many of these images will be useful in the future. For example, if you are going to make a film about Iranian tourist attractions, you can easily retrieve various films you have taken over the years and begin to edit them.

<< 44 >>

Follow your personal dreams

This journey has its own beauties and pleasures. We should not deprive ourselves from enjoying them and only keep destination in mind. Getting to destination without enjoying the beauties and also the hardships involved along the way is not pleasant. You can be rest assured you'll reach your dreams and if that's the goal then you have to take the right path and avoid deviating from it so you reach the desired destination. We must pinpoint our goals. The path is long and it's natural we get tired and decide to stop somewhere in line. But we should not regret anything and just keep on going with patience. Our survival is to go forward not to halt or turn back. We will reach our goal if we go forward, but by turning back we can never start again because the time has been lost, and unfortunately, time is the only thing that cannot be compensated or reversed. If you feel you are on the right track, try your best to the end and reach your goals and dreams, although this road has no end. You are considered successful just by moving and trying. For me, the real concept of success is that I have taken pleasure from doing what I do.

Nobody will hand you success if you sit at home

and do nothing. You need to work hard to achieve it. Trying is not hard rather needs patience. One has to be organized and go forward by planning. Do not be afraid of the unknown by closing your eyes in the hope of enlightenment, rather start the fire yourself and create the light. Dreams are the goals you like to achieve for brighter future. Stop dreaming about vain fantasies and think about real and achievable dreams. For sure if you stay in the queue with patience, success will eventually come to you. But if you always leave the queue unfinished and join another you can never go back to the beginning and your turn will never come. Our problem is often that we rush things and expect to reach everything quickly and effortlessly. So, we give up and nag as soon as the impossible is reached. Such people don't get anywhere, they constantly keep moving from this to that and blame others for our negligent and thoughtlessness. It is best to avoid the negative energy such people spread so you don't get disappointed and dodge work. The art of cinema is acquisitive and nobody has inherent talent for it, rather it is created through practice, interest, love and passion. The more we keep trying to gain experience the more knowledge is gained and better work is created.

<< 45 >>

Transfer your experiences to others

You are a self-taught filmmaker, and you definitely know by now that this art cannot be taught. You should discover the mysteries yourself. Techniques can be learned in any way and from anyone, but the art of cinema must be experienced. You will be able to achieve personal cinema by gaining various experiences through practice. In this path, you eventually meet those who are interests and want to learn cinema art like you. It is very enjoyable to pass on your experiences and by doing so; you will pave the way for others who are willing to make good use of your experiences. You can organize small workshops with one or more people and share the lessons you learned and tell them to learn from your experiences. But they must be willing to experiences new and fresh ideas. You have some personal experiences that only you acquired and are your personal knowledge. So it feels cool to share them with novices and anyone interested in filmmaking. Your experiences may light up their path so they can move on faster and easier.

www.ingramcontent.com/pod-product-compliance
Lightning Source LLC
Chambersburg PA
CBHW071409220526
45469CB00004B/1219